ACTI !

U-BOAT WAR RS

ACTION STATIONS!

U-BOAT WARFARE IN THE CLYDE IN TWO WORLD WARS

Alastair Alexander

Neil Wilson Publishing
www.nwp.co.uk

Opposite title page. A wartime convoy in mid-Atlantic under the watchful protection of the Royal Navy. (Copyright *Daily Record*).

First published by
Neil Wilson Publishing Ltd
0/2 19 Netherton Avenue
GLASGOW
G13 1BQ

Tel: 0141 954 8007
Fax: 0560 150 4806
E: info@nwp.co.uk
W: www.nwp.co.uk

A catalogue record of this book is available from the British Library.

ISBN: 978-1-906476-07-6
First published in October 2009
Reprinted April 2010, December 2010

Designed by Mark Blackadder

Printed by Bell & Bain, Glasgow

Dedication

To my daughters Shirley, Joyce and Susan, son-in-law Mark and my grandchildren Alexandra and Callum.

I would also like to thank my friend Cameron Houston for his encouragement, support and typing skills in completing the task.

CONTENTS

33

INTRODUCTION

At the beginning of the First World War in August 1914, Germany had about 20 operational U-boats in its High Seas Fleet. They were commanded by Korvettenkapitän Hermann Bauer. Their forward base was the fortified island of Heligoland, and within two days of war being declared a daring raid on the British Grand Fleet at Scapa Flow was attempted, but it was an abject failure with four U-boats being lost without sinking a single British ship.

The U-boat war resulted in 178 German losses with nearly 5,000 men killed. On the Allied side some 12 million tons of shipping (over 5,000 vessels in total) had been sunk with the loss of 15,000 lives. In October 1918, as the Great War neared its end, the Germans made a final, bold, but eventually futile attack.

UB116,[1] under the command of Oberleutnant zur See Emsmann, with a volunteer crew of 34 officers penetrated Hoxa Sound at Scapa Flow once again to attack the Grand Fleet. The boat was detected by hydrophones and sunk by mines. Germany was in the process of negotiating an armistice as this final attempt on Scapa Flow was made.

Twenty-one years later these exploits were not forgotten by Karl Dönitz, commander of the Kreigsmarine U-Boat Fleet, and on the 14th October 1939 U-47 commanded by Kapitänleutnant Günther Prien succeeded in entering Scapa Flow and sank the HMS *Royal Oak*, with a loss of 800 lives to give Germany a major propaganda victory right at the start of the war.

On the back of this success Dönitz turned his attention to the Clyde in an attempt to cripple or sink a major capital warship by laying mines in the inner Firth if possible.

1 During WWI 'UB' and 'UC' were submarine 'types'. During WWII, all were simply U-boats.

Opposite: U-33. (Copyright National Maritime Museum)

CHAPTER 1: 1914–18

In February 1915, a key decision was made by the German High Command. With the First World War now six months old, the seas around the British Isles were declared a War Zone and any ship found there after 18th February faced sinking without warning. Unrestricted U-boat warfare began for the first time in history.

UC-27

Three weeks later on the 11th of March, UC-27 under the command of Kapitänleutnant Bernd Wegener struck the first blow in the Clyde, for Kaiser and Reich, by sinking HMS *Bayano* (a 3,500-ton Elders & Fyffe banana boat converted into an armed merchant cruiser) a few miles off Corsewall Point, Galloway, with a loss of 200 of her crew.

Under the command of Captain Carr, the *Bayano* was returning to sea to resume her patrol duties. At 4.45am two thirds of her crew were asleep when without warning, she was hit amidships by a torpedo from UC-27. The initial explosion was quickly followed by several more as the ship's magazine detonated and within minutes the *Bayano* sank by her bow, accompanied by further underwater explosions. Captain Carr and many of his crew perished with only 50 survivors rescued. The first vessel on the scene was the collier SS *Castlereagh* of Belfast. The captain stopped his engines and attempted to pick up the survivors, but was alerted by the approach of a U-boat, in all probability the same UC-27. Restarting his engines, he set off at full speed on a zig-zag course pursued by the U-boat. After a dramatic 20-minute chase, the *Castlereagh* managed to escape and safely reached port to prevent UC-27 from adding a second prize.

Bernd Wegener was born in 1884 and entered, as a Seekadett, in the Kaiserliche Marine in 1903. He was promoted to Kapitänleutnant and given command of UC-27 in 1914, one of four U-boats of this type. Built at the Kaiserliche Werft, Danzig, she was commissioned on 8th May 1914 and Wegener took command on 1st August 1914, three days before First World War hostilities commenced. As part of the IV Flotilla he had his first success in action

Opposite. Winston Churchill, First Lord of the Admiralty, accompanied by his wife Clementine, arriving for the launch of HMS *Iron Duke* at Cammell Laird Portsmouth on 12th October 1912 (Copyright *Daily Record*)

1914–18: Single boom defence from Dunoon to Cloch Lighthouse with two attendant guard ships and the statue of Highland Mary in foreground. (Copyright James Hall Collection @ Norman Burniston)

within three months in the North Sea, sinking the British submarine E3. This was the first decisive action between submarines in the First World War.

Wegener was awarded the Iron Cross 1st Class for his exploits. In the course of three patrols in over 12 months, UC-27 sank 11 ships amounting to 32,385 tons and one warship HMS *Hermes* (5,600 tons) so Bernd Wegener was a dangerous and bold enemy. However, he was finally sunk by a British Q ship, HMS *Baralong* commanded by Lieutenant Godfrey Herbert RN on the 19th August 1915 in the Western Approaches near the Isles of Scilly at 50° 25' N, 08° 15' W.

UC-27 had stopped the SS *Nicosian* (with a full cargo of mules destined for the British Army in France) and was about to sink her, unaware of the approach of the British decoy ship. At 600 yards range *Baralong* engaged the enemy and fired 34 rounds which quickly sank the German submarine. About a dozen survivors swam to the *Nicosian* and fearful that they would try to sink the ship, Herbert ordered his Royal Marines to open fire; a number were killed but four managed to get on board and disappeared below. An armed boarding party from *Baralong* tracked them down to the engine room where they refused to surrender and were subsequently shot dead.

Wegener was shot and killed in the water as he tried to lead his remaining crew to board the *Nicosian*. The German government was outraged at the incident and demanded that the British officers be tried for murder. This was immediately rejected by the British government.

UC-27 MITTEL U CLASS SUBMARINE

Displacement: 971 tons gross
Length: 64.7m
Beam: 6.32m
Draught: 3.48m
Power: 2,000 hp (surface), 1,200 hp (submerged)
Speed: 16.4 knots (surface), 9.8 knots (submerged)
Range: 9,770 miles at 8 knots (surface) 85 miles at 5 knots (submerged)
Torpedoes: 6

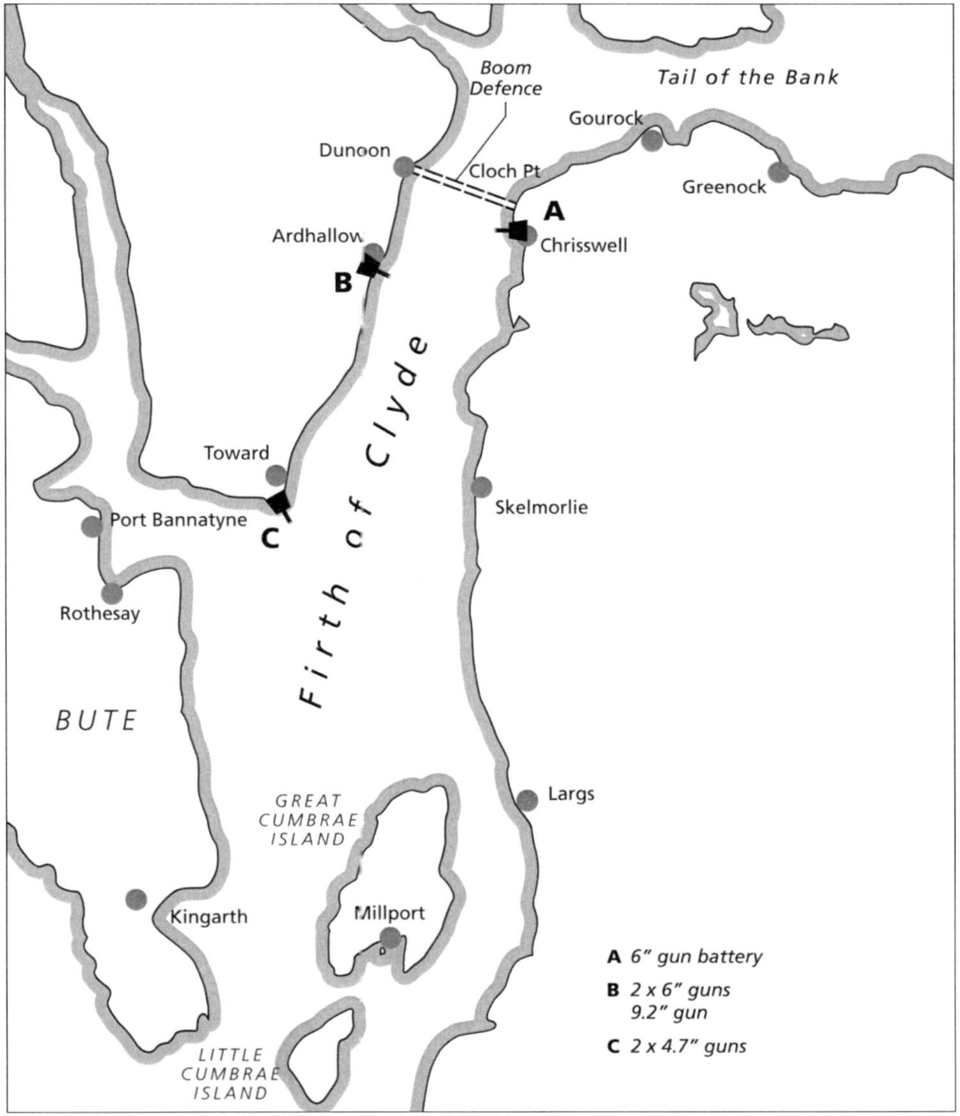

Deck Gun: 105mm/300 rounds
Crew: 35
Max Dive Depth: 50m/164ft
(Source: U-Boat Archive, Cuxhaven)

UC-75

It was not until November 1917 that the Kaiser's U-boat fleet claimed its second success in the Clyde, close to the site of the sinking of HMS *Bayano* in 1915, north of Corsewall Point. *Longwy*, a 1,323-ton French cargo vessel, met its end on the 4th November off the Galloway coast as UC-75, commanded by Oberleutnant Johannes Lohs, picked off the unescorted French ship. Details of the incident are unknown, as are the number of casualties of the French crew.[2]

Johannes Lohs was born on 24th June 1889 at Einsiedel, Sachsen, and entered the Kaiserliche Marine on 1st April 1909. He served aboard the cruiser *Strasburg* and saw action for the first time on 28th August 1914. He was moved to the U-Bootschule and gained his first command, UC-75 of the Flanderen Flotilla, on 17th March 1917. He led nine patrols off the British coast including a productive visit to the Clyde in early November 1917. By January 1918, his qualities as a U-boat commander were recognised and his award of the Iron Cross 1st Class in December 1917 was well merited. His ideas on U-boat warfare and a new tactical approach brought its reward with the award of the

2 See page 33 for sinking positions of *Bayano* and *Longwy*.

Opposite top. HMS *Bayano*, a converted auxiliary cruiser sunk by UC-27 on 11th March 1915 off Corsewall Point, Galloway.

Opposite below. SMS *Hindenburg*, battlecruiser, 30,700 tons with eight 12in guns, capable of 26 knots and one of three Derfflinger Class. She was the last battlecruiser built for the Imperial German Navy and the last ship to be scuttled at Scapa Flow at 5.00pm on 21st June 1919.

This page, far left. British Cavalry Unit on board ship on their way to France in August 1914.
(Copyright *Daily Record*)

Top left. SMS *Bayern*, battleship, 32,200 tons with eight 15in guns, capable of 22 knots and one of four Bayern Class battleships, She was scuttled at Scapa Flow on 21st June 1919.

Bottom left. The scuttling of the German High Seas Fleet at Scapa Flow in 1919 after surrender.
(Copyright *Daily Record*)

German High Seas Fleet arriving at Scapa Flow to surrender in June 1919.

Pour le Mérite on 24th April 1918. His last patrol from Zeebrugge was in charge of UB-57 and began on 3rd August 1918 as three ships were dispatched to the bottom in the Channel area: *Clan McVey* (5,815 tons) *Glenlee* (4,915 tons) and the *City of Brisbane* (7,094 tons). On returning to base, however, it is believed UB-57 hit a mine and all hands were lost. Lohs' body was washed ashore and was buried with full military honours at Vlissingen. UB-57 was presumed lost in a field of magnetic mines laid by the 20th Destroyer Flotilla off Zeebrugge at 51° 56' N, 02° 02' E. She was first submarine to be sunk by a magnetic mine.

In Lohs' short career he sank 76 merchant ships (147,075 tons), one warship (1200 tons) and a further 15 ships were damaged (85,420 tons).

UC-75, later commanded by Oberleutnant zur See Walter Schmitz, met her fate on 31st May 1918 off the east coast of England at 53° 57' N, 00° 09' E as she was rammed and sunk by HMS *Fairy* while attacking a convoy. Schmitz

German submarine fleet at Wilhelmshaven 1914.

survived along with 13 of his crew while 19 died in the action. However, the *Fairy's* bows had been badly damaged in the two rammings and she eventually sank without loss.

UC-75 MITTEL CLASS SUBMARINE

Displacement: 1150 tons gross
Length: 69.90m
Beam: 6.30m
Draught: 3.79m
Power: 2,300hp (surface), 1,240hp (submerged)
Speed: 16.8 knots (surface), 10.3 knots (submerged)
Range: 7,378 miles at 8 knots (surface) 115 miles at 6 knots (submerged)
Torpedoes: 12
Deck Gun: 88mm/264 rounds
Crew: 36
Max Dive Depth: 50m/164ft
(Source: U-Boat Archive Cuxhaven)

CHAPTER 2: 1939–45

With war being declared on 3rd Sept 1939 between Britain and Germany, the Clyde again resumed its position as a strategic location in the war effort. Following the daring assault on Scapa Flow by U-47 by Kapitänleutnant Günther Prien on the 13th October, in which he sank the 33,000-ton First World War battleship HMS *Royal Oak* with the loss of 800 lives, the Admiralty took the decision to disperse the Home Fleet from its Northern base until such times as its defences could be made secure from further U-boat attack.

Loch Ewe on the West Coast and the Tail of the Bank at Greenock on the Firth of Clyde could provide safe anchorages for the capital ships of the Royal Navy such as *Warspite, Barham, Nelson, Rodney,* and the flagship, the battlecruiser, HMS *Hood.* But German eyes were also on the Clyde, Konteradmiral Karl Dönitz, commander of the U-boat fleet wrote in his war log on 15th November 1940:

Radio intelligence reports have provided the following information on the whereabouts of the British Battlefleet.

a) The fast Battleshipships and Battlecruisers and several Aircraft Carriers are not in home waters but on special operations (chasing pocket battleships or escorting particular valuable convoys from Canada).

b) The major part of the remaining battleships apparently use mainly the Firth of Clyde as an anchorage. The question of a U-Boat action here against the English fleet has been considered and the following conclusions:

a) U-Boats cannot attack the anchorages themselves, the ships are laying in a long narrow strip of water to which is closed by a Boom.

b) It would be quite possible for U-boats to penetrate into the wider part of the Firth as far as the Boom there is a shallow position here, exactly on the main route, where mines could be laid.

This operation must be carried out as soon as possible, there is a good chance of catching large warships. It will however be necessary to use mines of a greater explosive effect than the TMB, as these cannot be guaranteed to sink if laid at this depth.

Opposite. 1939–45: Double boom defence from Cloch Lighthouse to Dunoon with seven attendant guard ships. (Copyright James Hall Collection @ Norman Burniston)

Right. Fairfields fitting-out basin, Glasgow circa 1929.
Left to right: *Arandora Star* built by Cammell Laird being refitted in Glasgow (14,694t and 512ft long). She was torpedoed by U-47, 2nd July 1940. HMS *Norfolk* (9,975t and 630ft long). RMS *Empress of Canada* (21,517t and 653ft long) built at Fairfields in 1920. She was torpedoed by an Italian submarine on the 13th March 1943 (Copyright *Daily Record*).

Opposite. Karl Dönitz congratulating the crew of U-47 after their successful sortie to Scapa Flow in October 1939 where HMS *Royal Oak* was sunk. (Photograph courtesy of Imperial War Museum London HU 40217)

The setting must be sufficiently coarse for them not to be exploded by the many merchant vessels, which ply these waters. The operation cannot be carried out until the mines have been manufactured.

c) If the Fleet sails north from the Clyde, it will be bound by navigational considerations.

U-Boats might operate with success along their route. The only question is when will the fleet sail? As long as it has nothing to do off the entrance to the North Sea, this is entirely uncertain. This can only be effected by operations by our own Battleships.

The operation of a lot of U-Boats against the Home Fleet in the Firth of Clyde therefore only promises to be worthwhile if it is carried out in co-operation with our own surface forces.

Group Command informs that Naval War Staff have

agreed to operations of Battleships beyond the line Shetlands-Norway as long as the British Fleet is in the Clyde and that such an operation is being planned for the next few days, it appears however, that it is impossible to postpone this even for a few days, which would be necessary to prepare the U-Boats and get them to their positions. If it could only have been postponed for 4 days a total of 11 U-Boats would have been available. On the date fixed on the other hand only 3–4 boats can be sent. A similar operation will therefore have to be planned for a later date. If it is planned long enough in advance the rest of the U-Boat war will not suffer to any extent.

The date must be chosen to fit in with the sailing times of the U-Boats, so that they will only have to be kept back for a few days and at the worst if the operation falls through, they can go on their operations areas for the war against merchant shipping.

(Source: F.d.U./B.d.U War Log. 1-15th November 1939 PG 30251)

If a mine-laying operation could be successfully carried out in the Clyde as well as hoping to sink or disable a large capital warship, there was the added bonus of trapping the largest ship in the world, the 83,000-ton RMS *Queen Elizabeth*, then nearing completion at Clydebank.

General policy for Mine laying Operations by U-Boats

1) Minefields should be laid at as many vital points as possible in order to cause a general interruption and dislocation of shipping.
2) Places reached by narrow channels must be blocked by several fields so that they will be unusable for a long period.
3) The inner areas must be mined before the outer approaches in order that a subsequent minelayer will not be prejudiced.
4) The mines must be laid at a depth at which they will destroy. War experience has shown that for the TMB mine to be effective, it should be used in a depth not exceeding 25 metres.

In November 1939, a new ground mine with a much heavier charge was devised and two new TMC type mines, with a charge of 1,000kg are ready for testing.

Blücher-Brücke

CHAPTER 3: FAILED ATTACK

U-32 FAILED MISSION

U-32 completed her second war patrol before returning to Wilhelmshaven on the 30th September 1939. Thereafter the boat went to Keil for repairs and a refit and it wasn't until the 28th December that she sailed on her minelaying operation to the Clyde, as authorised by Donitz. En route, on the evening of the 31st December, she torpedoed and sank the SS *Luna* (959t) West of Hagesund, Norway: a propitious start to her new mission.

The FdU[3] War Log records Dönitz's comments:

> 5.1 U-32 off the Clyde, according to dead reckoning nothing to report.

Then on the 8th January, the War Log notes:

> U-32 reports that she cannot carry out her mine laying operation off the Clyde. She has observed fixed listening stations and encountered strong patrols. She has not apparently succeeded in penetrating the INNER FIRTH. She also reports traffic observed close inshore south of Ailsa Craig Island, at water depths at which mines could be laid. She suggested making the alternative position and has been given orders to carry out the operation there. Until I hear the commanding officer's verbal report I shall not be satisfied that the first operation was really impossible.

By the 10th January U-32 reported further:

> She had carried out her operations in the alternative position. She has been allocated an operation area off the east coast of England for her remaining torpedoes.

Twelve days later after a 25-day patrol, U-32 entered port and the War Log notes tersely:

3 Fuhrer der Unterseaboote (Commander of Submarines).

Opposite. U-33 beside submarine tender at the Blücher Brude, Wilhelmshaven, circa 1939.

> She carried out her mine laying operation and also sank a steamer of 800-1000 tons in the North Sea. The commanding officer's (Paul Büchel) explanation of why he thought the minelay could not be carried out in the Clyde is not convincing. He pressed a long way forward and then turned back when he was in the midst of anti-S/M forces and only a few miles from the position in which he was to lay the mines, although he himself did not think he had been detected. He did not make an attempt on another day.
>
> The operation was a difficult one — too difficult of this C.O. I shall arrange for another boat to carry it out.
>
> Source: BdU[4] War Log 1-15th January 1940 PG 30255

U-32 was chosen for the mine laying operation in the Clyde after the Mining and Barrage Directorate promised Dönitz a full load of eight TMC mines would be ready for U-32 to lay by 10th December 1939. In fact U-32 did not sortie until the 28th December due to mechanical difficulties. It was significant that U-32 was unable to sail on her original planned date. She effectively lost three days because of a lack of skilled labour and a faulty exhaust valve. She eventually arrived off the Clyde on the 5th January, the same day as HMS *Hood* returning from patrol, entered the Clyde.

If U-32 had been in position three days earlier they would have had time to set up a planned torpedo attack after a successful mine laying operation, and the course of the war could have been changed. Dönitz now had to revise his plans, despite putting U-32 in perfect position to attack HMS *Hood* by either mines or torpedoes, the vigilance and strength of the British anti-submarine forces created indecision in the mind of Commander Paul Büchel, and the original plan was aborted.

Büchel was an experienced submariner, born on the 3rd August 1907 in Griefenberg, Pomerania and graduated in Crew 25 at Kiel. He took command of U-32 (Type VIIA) on 16th August 1937 when he was 30 and remained in command until 11th February 1940 when Dönitz effectively removed him from active service duties because of his failure to press home the planned mine laying operation in the Clyde.

It was not until 12th August 1943, that Fregatten Kapitan Paul Büchel received another command, due to rising losses in the Atlantic battle. U-860, newly commissioned Type IXD2, carried out only one patrol, sank no ships or damaged any and then was sunk on 15th June 1944 in the South Atlantic off St Helena by depth charges and rockets from seven Avenger and Wildcat aircraft from escort carrier USN *Solomons* resulting in 42 dead and 20 survivors. Paul Büchel survived and was among those taken prisoner. Her sinking position was on the South Atlantic, south of St Helena at 25° 27' S, 05° 30' W.

4 The title of FdU was changed to BdU (Oberbefehlshaber der Unterseeboote) on 19th September 1939.

The *Empress of Britain* and HMS *Hood* anchored off Princes Pier, Greenock after the largest convoy ever arrived in the Clyde in June 1940. Four months later the *Empress* was sunk by U-32. She was the largest merchant ship lost in the war. In May 1941 the *Hood*, Britain's largest warship, was sunk by the *Bismarck*. (Photograph courtesy of Imperial War Museum London H 497)

But what of U-32? When Paul Büchel was stripped of command he was immediately replaced by Hans Jenisch. On the 12th February 1940 he became the Commanding Officer, the third and last, in the lifetime of the vessel. Commissioned on the 15th April 1937 she was to meet her end in the Atlantic on 30th October 1940. Four days prior to this a German long-range bomber (Focke-Wulf Kondor 200C of 2/KG40) piloted by Lt Bernhard Jope took off from Mérignac near Bordeaux in France and while on patrol, sighted a large three-funnelled vessel steaming eastward 90 miles off the Irish Coast. It was the 42,000-ton Canadian-Pacific liner *Empress of Britain*, sailing on her own at 22 knots bound for Liverpool. She was immediately attacked and hit amidships and near the stern. Within half an hour, the ship was uncontrollably ablaze and Captain Sapsworth gave the order to abandon ship. She had been carrying 645 passengers and crew, 150 service personnel and their families.

A rescue operation was mounted and two destroyers, *Echo* and *Burza*, units of the Polish Navy, were detached from an inbound troop convoy. Three tugs were also despatched: *Thames* and *Marauder* from Campbeltown on the Mull of Kintyre, while *Seaman* left Londonderry and the 4,000-ton Carlisle Class cruiser HMS *Cairo* left Greenock to boost anti-aircraft cover. It wasn't until late in the afternoon that the last of the crew and passengers were evacuated from the stricken liner, now abandoned but floating on an even keel. More destroyers arrived on the scene; *Broke* and *Sardonyx* sent parties aboard the liner to secure hawsers for the tugs and by 13.00 it was reported the tow was under way at five knots.

It seemed that a miracle rescue was just possible, but cruelly just 13 hours later at 02.05 on the 28th October, the *Marauder* reported that the *Empress* had rolled over and sunk in under 10 minutes after two explosions on her port side. Lookouts reported sightings of what looked like two torpedo trails, but they were not confirmed. The liner sank north-west of the Aran isles off the west coast of Ireland. There were 598 passengers and crew rescued but there were 47 fatalities.

It was U-32 under the command of Oberleutnant Hans Jenisch that had administered the coup de grâce, and claimed the honour of sinking the largest merchant ship in the Battle of the Atlantic. He was awarded the Knights Cross for his success, but only had two days to savour it because the Royal Navy's response was swift and sure. On the 30th October, U-32 spotted a convoy straggler SS *Balzac*, and surfaced to sink her by shell fire, but the doughty freighter was able to escape after her distress calls were answered by two Tribal Class 1,400 ton destroyers, HMS *Harvester* and HMS *Highlander* who raced to her aid. *Harvester* manoeuvred to maintain ASDIC contact on the now submerged U-32, while *Highlander*, commanded by William Dallmeyer, set down an accurate pattern of depth charges which seriously damaged the U-Boat, forcing her to surface. Jenisch gave the order to abandon ship. By this time the main and secondary armament on the *Highlander* was in action and a number of the U-Boat crew were killed.

In total 37 survivors were picked up including Jenisch while six were killed, before the stricken U-32, caught in the searchlight beam, sank slowly, stern first, under the cold grey waters of the Atlantic. Its sinking position was north west of Ireland at 55° 37' N, 12° 20' W.

CHAPTER 4: LAST MISSION

U-33

Dönitz now turned his attention to U-33, another type VIIA submarine, chosen for her commanding officer, Hans Wilhelm von Dresky, born on 27th January 1908 in Halle un der Saale. He graduated in Crew No 29 from naval college and his first command as Kapitänleutnant was U-4 (type IIA) serving from September 1937 until October 1938 then transferring to U-33 on 29th October 1938. Dönitz, a committed Nazi, had picked Dresky not only for his experience at U-Boat handling skills, but also for his commitment to the National Socialist cause. It was now approaching the end of January and time was of the essence.

By the 4th February all preparations had been made for the patrol. Dönitz himself came to Wilhelmshaven harbour to see U-33 off, an unusual event for the Commander of the U-Boat arm. 'Good luck, Hans, look after yourself!' he shouted, as the 626-ton submarine left its moorings and eased out of the harbour. The crew knew how important their mission was, some even jesting with black humour that it was a suicide mission.

Indeed, the night before a banquet had been given for the crew, probably to boost their morale. In a wooden hut in a forest, food and drink was in abundance, and a number of girls had been laid on. As was customary, before going on patrol they put their civilian clothes and other personal mementoes into a tin box, each one of which would be sent to their next of kin in the event of the U-33 failing to return.

On the 5th February 1940 the War Log laconically records:

> U-28 and U-33 left Wilhelmshaven for Heligoland to make trial runs etc and will proceed from there to their operations areas.

But all was not well on U-33. While loading supplies at Wilhelmshaven, the bow slipped under the surface and freezing seawater poured in through an open torpedo hatch. Only prompt action by an alert crewmember (who blew all the water out of the diving tanks) averted what could have been a major problem. En-route to Heligoland, a fortified island off the German coast on which were stationed the Port Protection Flotilla, Port Commander and a naval fitting-out base, engineers had discovered two flaws which had appeared. There was a small hole in one of the torpedo tubes and a second hole in a copper pipe, possibly caused by a drill.

Temporary repairs were carried out until they reached Heligoland where permanent repairs could be completed by key civilian workers to satisfy Chief Engineer Friedrich Schilling who had the final say as to whether U-33 was in a fit state for the mission.

You're safe now! The Navy's here! After being adrift for eight days 46 survivors including six children are picked up and taken ashore to Greenock. (Copyright James Hall Collection @ Norman Burniston)

On the 7th February there is a brief entry in the War Log:

> U-33 left Heligoland in accordance with order No 24.

While U-33 made her way northwards, navigating round the Northern Isles, then west of the Hebrides before approaching the Clyde area. Her top speed would have been 16 knots on the surface and eight knots submerged. On the 9th February, HMS *Hood* and HMS *Warspite*, escorted by eight destroyers, left Greenock to give cover to Scandinavian convoys. Between the 12th and 14th February the battle group was on patrol north-west of Shetland. A foray east was made to support the boarding of the *Altmark* if necessary, before returning to Greenock on 18th February.[5]

U-Boat HQ were preoccupied over this period with operations against HMS *Ark Royal*, *Renown* and *Exeter* which were sailing from Freetown in West Africa after taking part in the hunting down of the German pocket battleship *Graf Spee* and Dönitz was preparing to set an ambush for the British task force. The chief radio intelligence station expressed the view that a channel port was probably the destination, but Dönitz was unsure where to position U-26, 37 and 48. War Log entry of the 12th February:

5 The *Altmark* was a German supply vessel that was boarded by the Royal Navy in neutral Norwegian waters on the 16th February 1940.

> Radio Intelligence has reports of a sinking of a U-Boat in the Clyde. If this is correct, it can only be U-33, but the reports are not so definite, that hope of the boat only having been seen, need not be abandoned.

Dönitz must have feared the worst for U-33, but he had no time to reflect, because the Commander in Chief of the German navy, Erich Raeder, visited Headquarters West that day and Dönitz had to brief him on the situation and future plans.

It was also reported that *Ark Royal* with her escort of four destroyers was making for the Channel. Of the three German submarines in the operational war zone only U-37 was strategically positioned. U-48 was not able to take up position because she was trying to attack a convoy and U-26, with an inexperienced captain in command, was in danger of running out of fuel.

Dönitz must have been frustrated, with the possible loss of U-33 still to be confirmed and the opportunity of sinking a Royal Navy capital ship within his grasp. War Log entry of the 15th February:

> ARK ROYAL, RENOWN and EXETER have arrived at the Channel Ports. U-37 therefore required new orders.

It was later confirmed that probably by the evening of the 13th February *Ark Royal* was in Portsmouth while *Renown* and *Exeter* entered Plymouth at 08.00 hours on the 15th February. It was not until the 16th February, that Dönitz had his worst fears confirmed.

> It seems more and more likely that U-33 has been lost. Several radio intelligence reports that she was in action with an English Minesweeper and they surrendered. Assistance was requested to rescue survivors, the English authorities assumed that mines had been laid, this is not improbable, as their events took place in the early morning hours. The U-Boat would certainly not have chosen this time to penetrate into the Clyde and she then at least would have been on the way out. If she really did lay the mines, the high price paid will have been worth it[6]

In his memoir *Ten Years and 20 Days* first published in 1958, Dönitz gave his account of his career.[7] In it he devoted four pages to the success of U-47 and Prien in sinking the *Royal Oak* at Scapa Flow, while U-33 and Von Dresky is dismissed in one line:

> In operations in the Clyde, U-33 and her entire crew were lost.

6 Source: BdU War Log 1-15th February 1940.

7 The planned early mine offensive by Dönitz involved a total of 34 mining missions and the mines laid accounted for 115 ships totalling 395,000 tons. Prize victims were the battleship HMS *Nelson* at Loch Ewe by U-31 and the cruiser HMS *Belfast* in the Firth of Forth on the 4th December 1939 by mines laid by U-21. Both ships were out of service for a considerable period of time.

Schmid | W. Wilden
Keller | Patten
GERMAN NAVY
12. 2. 1940
L. Poppel | L. Wagner
Groß | Heckerodt
Albrecht | Kursiefen
P. Anger | P. Rausch
GERMAN NAVY
Bergfeld | W. Enders
K. H. Peters
GERMAN NAVY
12. 2. 1940
Ruhet sanft
1940

CHAPTER 5: THE SINKING OF U-33 BY HMS GLEANER

U-33 was under the command of Kapitänleutnant Otto Heinrich Junker from 25th July until 28th October 1938. From mid-1937 until October 1938 she carried out three patrols in Spanish Waters, aiding Franco's forces in the Spanish Civil War. Kapitänleutnant Kurt Freiwald shared duties with Junker during this period before Kapitänleutnant Hans Wilhelm Von Dresky assumed command on 29th October 1938.

When the war began U-33 (2nd Salzwedel Flotilla) had an aggressive and successful first patrol sinking three British coastal ships. The war was only four days old when the 4,000-ton *Olivegrove* was her first victim, followed by *Arkleside* (1,467 tons) and the smaller *Caldew* (287tons), before returning to Wilhelmshaven on the 27th September.

A second patrol, leaving port on 29th October, was set for a minelaying expedition in the Bristol Channel which was successfully completed on the 5th November. Now U-33 could turn her attention to the shipping lanes. There was frustration on the 16th November when she missed an opportunity to sink the SS *Hope Star* but a further seven British ships were not so lucky.

From the 20th to the 24th November U-33 sank a total of 18,735 tons to complete a highly successful patrol. Her victims were *Thomas Hankins* (276tons), *Delphine* (250 tons), *Sea Sweeper* (329 tons), *Sulby* (287 tons), *William Humphries* (276 tons) and *Borkum* (3,670 tons). The latter was a German prize ship being towed back to Orkney. The *Sussex* followed (13,647 tons) and U-33 returned in triumph to Wilhelmshaven on 26th November.

A third War Patrol from December 1939 to January 1940 saw U-33 sink the *Stanholme* (2,473 tons) on Christmas Day and her final victim proved to be the *Inverdargle* (9,456 tons). U-33 sent a total of 36,478 tons of British shipping to the bottom.

Von Dresky had proved his worth, but his fourth mission, to carry out the minelaying operation in the Clyde, was his downfall. U-33 entered the Clyde Estuary rounding the Mull of Kintyre after midnight on the 11th February intending to achieve a good positioning in the inner firth to lay their mines.

German POWs pay their respects to their countrymen who died when U-33 was sunk by HMS *Gleaner* in February 1940. This photograph was taken in 1946. The bodies were exhumed from Greenock Cemetery in 1962 and re-interred at the German Military Cemetery at Cannock Chase in Staffordshire. (Copyright James Hall Collection @ Norman Burniston)

Proceeding on the surface on a moonless night, their lookouts spotted a blacked-out vessel travelling in the opposite direction, it was HMS *Gleaner*, carrying out the westerly leg of her designated triangular patrol. U-33 continued her progress undetected, now submerged at periscope depth but on her return sweep *Gleaner*'s Asdic operator picked up a suspicious noise which sounded like a diesel engine.

The minesweeper put about, searchlights were switched on, and a white object, which could have been the spray from a periscope was sighted, but soon disappeared. At 3.53am a pattern of five depth charges were dropped, to devastating effect. On the sea bed at 36 metres beneath the surface Von Dresky took stock of the situation. One of the diesel motors wouldn't work, lights were out and many of the instruments were broken and worst of all, seawater was beginning to leak into the boat.

Over the next hour two more batches of depth charges exploded around them, worsening their situation, they found they were stuck on the seabed, and desperate measures were needed. At 5.22am the order was given to blow the tanks and U-33 began its ascent to the surface. The crew, wearing life jackets, were given the order to abandon ship as the submarine broke the surface. Von Dresky knew the time had come to set off the scuttling charges and to ensure that the vital Enigma machine was prevented from falling into the hands of the British. After two attempts they exploded and ensured U-33 would be scuttled before any possibility of capture. Von Dresky and three other engineers died in the process and their bodies were never recovered.

There were 17 survivors and 23 dead who perished of exposure and drowning in the Clyde. The dead were buried in Greenock Cemetery on the 16th February 1940 in six lairs (numbers 930-5) early in the morning on a cold and icy day. The lairs were purchased in the name of the king by Rear Admiral BC Watson. Twenty-two years later the bodies were exhumed and transferred to the German Military Cemetery at Cannock, Staffordshire and re-interred in Block 3, Row 11, lairs 326-346. The number of bodies transferred were 25 in total: 23 from U-33 and two other unknown German bodies buried on 5th July 1940 in adjoining lair No 931.

The wreck of U-33 is still largely intact despite the damage she sustained from the depth charges and the effects of her scuttling and after almost 70 years on the seabed, a small oil leak marks her position.

Max Schiller remained a prisoner of war until 1946, staying on in Scotland and marrying a local girl where they settled down to life on a farm. In 2000, he was given the opportunity of laying a wreath in the waters of the Clyde where U-33 sank. On board HMS *Cromer* a Royal Navy minehunter, the 78-year-old was able to pay tribute to his fallen comrades accompanied by the German Navy mine hunter *Vident*. Max Schiller died in 2002.

In his report to the Commander in Chief, Home Fleet, Lieutenant Commander HP Price details the actions taken by HMS *Gleaner* on the fateful morning of the 12th February 1940:

Sir, I have the honour to report the destruction of U-33 by HMS Gleaner under my command at 05.31GMT on Monday 12th February 1940.

2. [*sic*] On Sunday 11th February, while on Outer Patrol in the Firth of Clyde, with instructions to patrol in the vicinity of the 25 fathom contour between Ailsa Craig and Ship Rock Lighthouse, I instituted a tri-angular night patrol, at 8 knots in a clockwise direction between the following points,

A-213.5° distant 5.4 miles from Pladda Lighthouse.

B-194° distant 11.8 miles from Pladda Lighthouse.

C-228° distant 16.1 miles from Pladda Lighthouse.

For night patrol a listening watch only was kept with A/S gear, but orders were given to investigate with A/S beam any hydrophone effects heard and whilst on course BC to sweep occasionally with A/S beam to the southward.

3. At 02.50 hours on Monday 12th February, Sub Lieutenant E.P. Reade being on watch, the S.D. Rating AB W.J.T. Mellor O.N. SSX 23375, reported strong hydrophone effects bearing 205°. Ship was in position approx. 2 miles south of A steering 180° A/S beam was tried but contact was not obtained, the object being probably out of range. Sub Lieutenant Reade ordered the H.S.D rating Able Seaman H.T.Rhodes O.N. JX138069 to close up, brought the 4in to the ready, the depth charges to the ready and called me, he altered course to port towards the object at 02.57 and obtained contact with hand transmission at a range of about 3,000 yards.

4. On reaching the bridge I heard strong hydrophone effects on bearing 150° but no echo. The hydrophone noises were very loud and sounded rather like the noise of a diesel engine but at the rate of about two per second thus Tonk Tonk Tonk etc. I altered further to port so as to bring the H.E. slightly on the starboard bow, increasing speed gradually and at 03.16 hours was doing 16 knots bearing of contact was 030°, range approx. 3200 yds and own ship's head 030° from then onwards range decreased slowly, but fearing that the craft would escape I altered course to 360° to bring searchlight to bear. Contact bearing was rapidly drawing aft on starboard side now and searchlight was switched on, on a bearing of 070°. On a bearing of 115° an object which looked white and possibly the spray from a periscope was illuminated but almost at once disappeared. At 03.56 wheel was put over and ship swung rapidly to starboard to close object, telegraphs being put to full ahead.

5. Object was passed over at 03.40 but depth charges were not fired as A/S operator had trouble with the firing bar on recorder and was not ready to estimate time to fire the pattern.

It was considered best not to fire haphazardly owing to the time which would elapse before reloading could be completed. After passing object by about 800 yds wheel was put over to starboard and course altered by 180° to approx. 360° contact was again made and U-boat attacked at 03.53 when a pattern of 5 depth charges was fired by remote control from the bridge. One of the chutes failed to release and four charges only were actually dropped the one failing being the last of the pattern. All 4 charges exploded with good detonation being set with both throwers to 150 feet and all chutes to 100 feet on detonation, dynamo tripped, lights were extinguished gyro failed and A/S contact was temporarily lost.

6. At 04.12 a second attack was made but the only depth charge that was at the ready was that which had not been released in the first attack. This was because the re-loading party were finding it almost impossible to reload with the ship listing heavily from the effect of large helm movements at high speed. The depth charge detonated set to 100 feet and was fired as the centre one of a pattern. A non-sub contact was made at 04.27 and disregarded after investigation.

7. Contact was made again at 04.40 and the U-boat attacked with a pattern of 5 depth charges, set with throwers at 150 feet and chutes at 100 feet, all charges detonated well, and though dynamo remained unaffected lights were extinguished on Bridge and in instruments. Fuse of SEND-RECEIVE key burnt out giving 55 volts instead of 111 volts and S.R. Key failed to go over to Send. Loud Speaker was also slightly damaged and sensitivity of it became very low.
A/S gear was now completely out of action and a search was made with searchlight with ship circling the area at 12 knots. Searchlight would only burn for a few seconds at a time as carbons had been broken with the first charge and the breaker kept falling off.

The two 10in Signalling Projectors were brought into use and at 05.22 a U-boat on the surface was seen in the beam of the searchlight but temporarily lost on searchlight failing again. 4in gunfire was opened at 05.23, 5 rounds being fired, and Gleaner turned to ram, Crew of U-boat were seen to emerge on deck and hold up their hands in surrender, so wheel was put hard a starboard and engines to full astern, ship stopping parallel to U-boat at about one cable distance. At 05.30 a shower of sparks was seen coming from the Conning Tower and the crew abandoned U-boat, which at once trimmed by the bow and slowly disappeared without list developing an angle of tilt about 40°. Position of sinking of U-boat was approx. 150° distant 4.8 miles from Pladda lighthouse (Lat. 55° 25' N Long. 5° 07' W) this position could not be obtained accurately as bearings could only be taken with magnetic compass with the aid of a torch. HMS Scott who appeared on the scene later was requested to locate and buoy the wreck which sank in 30 fathoms of water heading northeast.

8. Port whaler was lowered and set away for survivors but ship was drifting to leeward so starboard whaler and both motor skiffs were not lowered until ship had steamed slowly to centre of largest group of men. Sea was very choppy and pulling boats could hardly make any headway against it. One officer and a rating were picked up by Gleaner's boats.

One officer was picked up by trawler Floradora and two officers and seven ratings by trawler Bohemian Girl, two of the latter ratings died whilst on passage to Lamlash, where in sheltered waters those in Bohemian Girl were transferred to Gleaner HMS Kingston picked up 22 men only 2 being alive.

HMS Scott arrived on the scene at 07.55 and permission was obtained for Gleaner to proceed to Greenock, where after calling at Lamlash, ship arrived at

12.50 on Monday 12th February and prisoners were transferred to Military Authorities.

9. Following appendices are attached-

a) Rough Diagram of courses of Gleaner and U-33.

b) List of survivors handed over to the Military Authorities by Gleaner together with 2 dead.

I have the honour to be,
Sir,
Your obedient servant,
Signed
Hugh P Price
Commander in Command.[8]

It was reported by the naval authorities that five mines had been laid by U-33 before her demise. The TMC mine had been tested on the 29th November 1939, it was 3.39m long and weighed 1,115kg of which 1,000kg was the warhead. Eight TMC mines would have been aboard U-33.

British radio traffic would have been monitored by B-Dienst[9] and if the Fleetwood trawler *Floradora* had reported the sighting of a mine on open frequency, this is how Dönitz would have gleaned his information that provided him with the hope that U-33 had actually completed her mission.

Von Dresky had done his best to ensure vital parts of the Enigma encoding machine would not fall into British hands as members of his crew had been ordered to drop

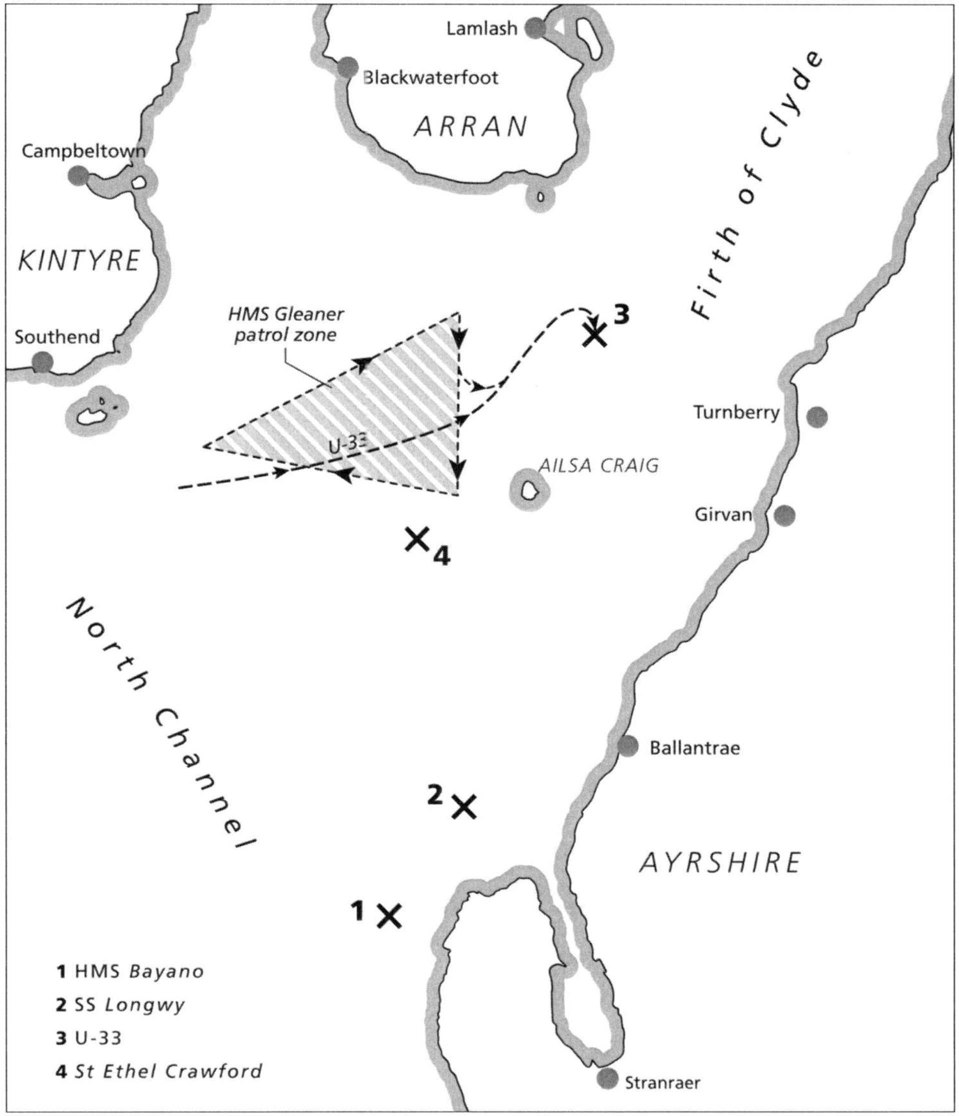

8 Source: National Archives File ADM 199/123.

9 Beobachtungsdienst. The German intelligence listening service.

into the Clyde key component parts of it as they emerged on deck. However, a few days later a Royal Navy ship, the Hunt Class minesweeper HMS *Tedworth*, was moored over the wreck and a team of divers were scouring the seabed recovering the rotors and other vital components. The divers also entered U-33 and carried out a further detailed search recovering more items of importance. The bodies of Von Dresky and the three crew members who went down with him remained undisturbed. This remarkable salvage operation was the first time any of the parts of an Enigma encoding machine had ever been recovered in wartime. It was an incident of huge significance as the materials were despatched in great secrecy to Bletchley Park in order to aid the cracking of the Enigma codes by the intelligence boffins.

The action by HMS *Gleaner* was also notable in that the sinking of U-33 was the first by Asdic and was a forerunner to many successes to come in the Battle of the Atlantic. The Director of Anti-Submarine warfare noted in the Official Report.

> This incident is of particular interest as it is the first known case in which the hunt has been conducted entirely by ASDICS – from internal detection to the surfacing of the U-Boat.[10]

One of the concerns of the BdU and KM staff officers was the danger of relatively large boats operating in shallow waters and the attendant risk of capture of cipher materials such as the Enigma rotors. It was decreed that for all future mine-laying operations after the 10th September 1939, U-Boats would land their most sensitive material, encoding their communications with the old-fashioned AFB hand cipher system.

Why U-33 sortied on her mission to the Clyde with her Enigma machine on board, especially when strict orders had been issued to the contrary, remains a mystery but probably explains why Von Dresky was desperate at all costs to scuttle his submarine to prevent the secret equipment falling into the hands of the Royal Navy. His diligence made him pay him the ultimate price.

List of 17 Survivors from U-33 sunk by HMS *Gleaner* 12th February 1940.

Friedrich Schilling – Kapitänleutnant
Karl Vietor – Oberleutnant Z See
Heinz Rottman – Oberleutnant (ing)
Johannes Becker – Leutnant Z See
Friedrich Kumpf – N101T/29 Stabsobermaschinist
Paul Galileia – N224/325 Bootsmann
Ernst Masanek – N882t/34 Obermaat
Heinz Marticke – N386/33 Haupgefreiter
Werner Siegert – N2414T/35 Haupgefreiter
Robert Puchta – N2708T/37 Obergefrieter
Heinz Krink – N3744T/37 Obergefrieter
Heinrich Weber – N2943/37S Obergefrieter

10 Source: National Archives File ADM 199/123. Admiralty: War History Cases and Papers: Second World War. Anti U-Boat operations reports and assessments 1940.

Peter Lingsheidt – N946/37S Obergefrieter
Ernst Scherer – N2724T/37 Obergefrieter
Han Joachim Ehrhardt – N2575T/383 Gefrieter
Manfred Krampe – N155T/38 Gefrieter
Max Schiller – N2602/32S Matrose

List of 23 dead from U-33 sunk by HMS *Gleaner* 12th February 1940.

Klinger	Werner Keller
Willhelm Wilden	Herbert Rath
Erich Palten	Heinz Karl Mohr
Karl Heinz Peters	Heinrich Liebert
Walter Kunik	Gustav Henneberg
Heinrich Kampert	Hans Bergfeld
Willibald Steiner	Werner Paul Enders
Paul Rausch	Heinrich Kursiefen
Paul Anger	Albrecht
Adalbert Heckerodt	Karl Gross
Leopold Poppel	Ludwig Wagner
Christian Schmid	

No other bodies were recovered. Von Dresky and three members of the crew, Friedrich Braun, Johannes Johne and August Winteroff went down with U-33.

Greenock Cemetery originally recorded that Max Schiller was one of the deceased, but this was an error over identity tags and Karl Heinz Peters was added to the list and Schiller was removed.

It would appear that Klinger and Albrecht were not part of the normal crew, and may have been technicians on board to supervise the first laying of the new TMC mine.

Total crew: 44
Survivors: 17
Dead: 27
Sinking position: North of Ailsa Craig at 55° 25'N 05° 07'W.

U-33
Type VII A Submarine
Commissioned 25th July 1936. Built by Germaniawerft, Keil. Laid down 1st September 1935.
Displacement: 626 tons (surface), 745 tons (submerged)
Length: 211m
Beam: 19m
Draught: 14m
Propulsion: diesel 2 x 2,320hp; electric 2 x 750hp.
Battery: 2 x 62
Fuel: 108 tons.
Speed: 16 knots (surface), 8 knots (submerged)
Range: 4,300 miles at 12 knots (surface), 90 miles at 4 knots (submerged)
Weapons: 4 x bow tubes, 1 x stern tube, 11 x torpedoes.
Mines: 22 x TMA or 33 x TMB. Guns: 1x 88mm, 1x 20mm.
Crew: 44
Diving depth (operational) 100m/328ft
Crush depth: 196m/645ft.
Number Built: 10

CHAPTER 6: THE LAST PATROL

U-218

In Europe the Second World War had 47 days remaining when U-218 under the command of Kapitänleutnant Rupprecht Stock left Bergen in Norway on what proved to be her last war patrol. The last of the type VII D submarines, she was commissioned on 24th January 1942 as part of the 8th Flotilla in Danzig and was fitted with a 'Snorchel' underwater breathing apparatus in May 1944; there were six of these specialised submarines commissioned between U-213 (August 30th 1941) and U-218.

Nearing the end of the patrol U-218 entered Clyde waters on the 17th April 1945 and proceeded to lay 13 SMA type mines in an area four miles south-west of Ailsa Craig, as she was unable to penetrate further due to vigilant Royal Navy anti-submarine patrol sweeps. Her work completed she was able to leave the Clyde area undetected and via the Western Approaches, made the return journey across the North Sea to Bergen just in time to surrender on the 8th May 1945. The deadly cargo she left behind, however, claimed the Kreigsmarine's final victim in the Clyde. On the 20th April the Aberdeen-registered *Ethel Crawford*, a 200-ton steam trawler owned by the Ardrossan Trawling Co. Ltd, struck one of the mines laid just two days earlier by U-218. There was a massive explosion and the trawler with her crew of 10, sank within minutes. There were no survivors. The vessel was originally built in 1919 by Scott & Co. of Bowling and named *John Langshaw* but later re-named *Ethel Crawford*. Her sinking position is given on the Admiralty Charts as 55° 13' N, 05° 14' W.

Kapitänleutnant Rupprecht Stock was born on 16th February 1916 in Frankfurt am Main. He was appointed Commander of U-214 in May 1943 based in Brest and carried out seven war patrols covering 275 days at sea, resulting in almost 20,000 tons of shipping sunk. In August 1944 Stock was transferred to U-218 based at Bergen and took her out on two patrols lasting 91 days.

Apart from the sinking of the *Ethel Crawford* the last patrol had one further sinking to add to its war record. On the 10th July 1945, two months after the war ended in

Opposite. HMS *Gleaner*, the Halcyon Class minesweeper, which sank U-33 on 12th February 1940 in the Clyde off Arran. (Photograph courtesy of Imperial War Museum London LF 4927)

9. (a) & (b) Two dramatic pictures a German Kondor Focke-Wulf 200c long-range bomber based in France attacking a British convoy and scoring a hit on a heavily laden freighter. It wasn't until escort carriers were built to protect the convoys that the ever-present danger of an air raid or submarine attack be prevented. (Copyright James Hall Collection @ Norman Burniston)

Europe, HMS *Kurd* (FY[11] 639, 352 tons) a requisitioned trawler used as a minesweeper struck a mine laid by U-218 some time previously. HMS *Kurd* under the command of Lieutenant Commander Roy Barrett RNR was sweeping mines off Cornwall and sank of Lizard Head; two officers and 14 ratings were lost while 11 survivors were picked up by HMS *Almandine* (FY 645). Her estimated sinking position was 49° 54' N 05°17' W. This was the last sinking of a British ship by U-Boat action in World War Two.

After surrender at Bergen on May 8th 1945, U-218 was transferred to Loch Ryan on the Clyde and as part of Operation Deadlight was sunk by the Royal Navy on 4th December 1945, 8.9 nautical miles off Inishtrabull, Northern Ireland in the deep waters of the North Channel.

U-218 TYPE VIID

Displacement: 965 tons (surface), 1,080 tons submerged
Length: 76.90m
Beam: 6.40m
Draught: 5m
Power: diesel 2 x 2,800hp; electric 2 x 750hp
Speed: 16 knots (surface), 7.3 knots (submerged)
Range: 8,100 miles at 12 knots (surface), 69 miles at 4 knots (submerged)
Weapons: 5 x 53.3 TT. Guns: 1 x 88mm, 1 x 20mm
Crew: 44
Diving depth: (operational) 100m/328ft
Crush depth: 200m/645ft.

11 Flotilla number

On 4th May 1945 all U-Boats at sea were ordered by the German High Command to cease hostilities and return to base, but due to poor communications only a few submarines received the signal and on the 7th May, U-2336 sank two ships south east of May Island in the Firth of Forth. The Canadian vessel *Avondale Park* (2,878 tons) and the Norwegian ship *Sneland 1* (1,791 tons). Under Kapitänleutnant Emil Klusmeier, U-2336 returned to Kiel on the 14th May to surrender to the Allied authorities. There was only one other case of a ship being sunk after the ceasefire; off Long Island USA. SS *Black Point* was torpedoed by U-853 on the 5th May but did not succumb until the 6th. The official end of the war came at midnight on the 8th May 1945.

Far left. A heavily laden cargo ship carrying aircraft on deck.
Above. All seems calm, but lurking U-boat Wolf Packs would wait for nightfall to get into the middle of the convoy to cause death and destruction.
Left. A Clyde-bound convoy on the alert in mid-Atlantic. In wartime the censor would have blocked out of the picture the advanced sights of the Bofors Gun. (Copyright James Hall Collection @ Norman Burniston)

Above. Roll out the barrel! Only this time it's depth charges.
Right. A Canadian Corvette crew go through their attack drill. Note the variety of headgear or lack of it. (Copyright James Hall Collection @ Norman Burniston)

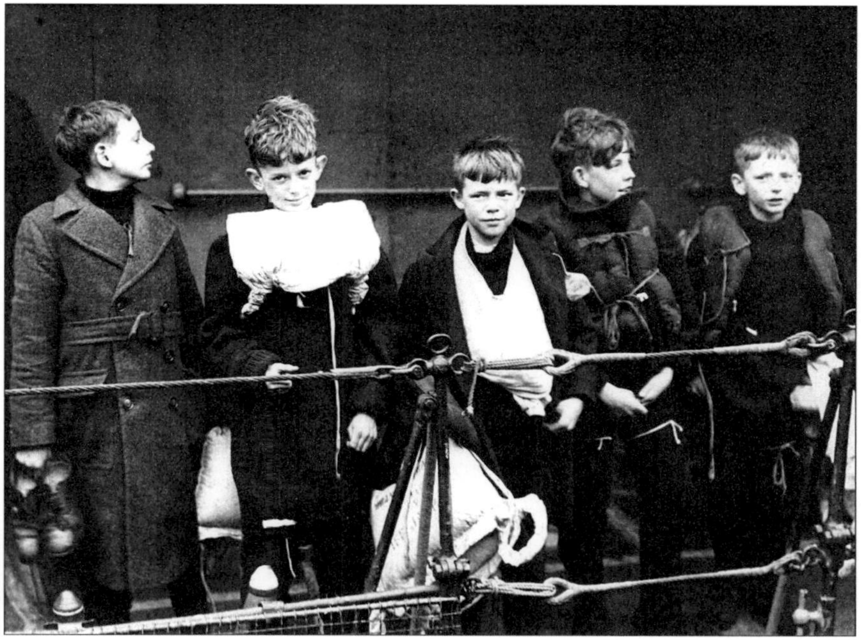

Left. Survivors of *City of Benares* picked up by Royal Navy HMS *Anthony* A-Class Destroyer (built at Scotts of Greenock) after being adrift in the Atlantic for eight days with 46 survivors including six children. (Copyright James Hall Collection @ Norman Burniston)

Above. Five children who were survivors of the sinking of the *City of Benares* sunk by U-48, 600 miles out in the Atlantic; 243 were killed including 77 evacuee children. (Copyright James Hall Collection @ Norman Burniston)

The inner area of the Firth of Clyde was never breached. The defence boom lay between the Cloch Lighthouse and the Dunoon side; a double barrier of heavy chain link providing an impenetrable wall to the Tail of the Bank anchorages. Seven guard vessels were on constant duty and on both sides of the river land-based listening and observation posts plus an ASDIC loop ensured total coverage. Coastal defence batteries were in fortified positions with a 6-inch gun battery at the Cloch Lighthouse and at Ardhallow on the Argyll side 2 x 6-inch guns plus a large 9.2-inch gun. At Toward Point 2 x 4.7-inch guns were well situated to cover the river. As VE day was celebrated the 11th Minesweeping Flotilla based at Ardrossan was given the task of clearing the Clyde of any remaining enemy mines. By the 18th July 1945 it was reported that 500 square miles of the Clyde estuary was all clear.

Opposite. Fitting-out basin at Fairfields Shipyard, Glasgow circa 1944. HMS *Theseus,* Colossus Class light fleet aircraft carrier (13,350t) 3no Battle Class Destroyers Cadiz, Camperdown and Finisterre (2,315t). (Copyright James Hall Collection @ Norman Burniston)

HMS *Geranium* (Flower Class corvette) built by Simons of Renfrew and launched on 23rd April 1940. Displacement 925 tons; top speed 16 knots; armament 1 x 4-in, 1 x 2 pdr AA or 0.5in AA, (1x4) 4 x 0.303in AA; complement 85. This type of ship (named *Compass Rose*) was used in the film *The Cruel Sea* starring Jack Hawkins. (Photograph courtesy of The Ballast Trust)

Convoy in the North Atlantic.
(Copyright *Daily Record*).

Left. American P47 Thunderbolt fighters are unloaded in Glasgow after their hazardous transatlantic journey. (Copyright *Daily Record*)

Above. Captain, chief engineer and second officer on standby on the bridge of their ship ready for another attack. (Copyright *Daily Record*)

SACRED
TO
THE MEMORY OF
THOSE NAMED
WHO LOST THEIR LIVES
IN
H.M. SUBMARINE K 13
IN THE
GARELOCH
29th JANUARY 1917
IN MEMORY OF
ALL ALLIED SUBMARINERS W.W.II
STILL ON 'PATROL'
BY
FAMILIES AND FRIENDS

CHAPTER 7: WARTIME LOSSES ON THE CLYDE

FIRST WORLD WAR

Trygon (289NT) Trawler
Built by Cook, Welton & Gemmell (Hull) launched 1908. Adapted for minesweeping duties by the Admiralty on the outbreak of war. Lost in a collision on 30th March 1915 the wreck lies in a position 55°29.783'N, 005°02.683' W in approx 60 metres of water.

K13 (2,650DT) K Class submarine.
Built by Fairfield Shipbuilding & Engineering Co Ltd Glasgow and launched on 11th November 1916. While undergoing acceptance trials in the Gareloch on 29th January 1917, on her second dive and with 80 on board, the submarine went into an uncontrolled descent eventually coming to rest on the bed of the loch in 64 feet of water. The hull was ruptured and with water pouring into various sections only 48 people managed to get into the sealed off area of the control room; the remaining 32 were drowned or suffocated by fumes. Frantic rescue operations were put in hand and divers managed to connect an airline to the control room area in order to provide fresh air to the trapped crew. Work was carried out to the forward ballast tanks to enable them to be blown and the stricken submarine was brought to the surface. Finally when holes were cut in the hull the survivors were rescued after over 50 hours underwater. The boat was towed back to the shipyard, re-fitted and re-commissioned as K22. The number 13 was never again given to a Royal Navy submarine. A memorial to the six Fairfield employees and 26 naval personnel who perished stands in Elderpark, Govan, Glasgow. Of the seven submarines to have sunk in the Firth of Clyde only one was lost through conflict (U-33), two by planned action and four by accident.

HMS *Ulysses* (1,090NT) U Class Destroyer.
Built by William Doxford & Sons, Sunderland. Launched March 1917. While on duty in the Clyde, *Ulysses* was in collision with the steamship *Ellerie* on 29th October 1918. Fortunately she sank without any loss of life. Due to wartime security her sinking position is unknown.

Opposite. Memorial to the men lost in HMS *K13* in the Gareloch on the 29th January 1917. Situated in Elderpark Glasgow.

CHAPTER 8: WARTIME LOSSES ON THE CLYDE

SECOND WORLD WAR

Maillé Brézé (2,441NT). French destroyer.
After providing escort to the troop convoys for the disastrous Norwegian campaign, she returned to the Clyde and was back at anchor off Princes Pier, Greenock, on 30th April 1940. Suddenly, during maintenance, one of her starboard torpedoes exploded accidentally. The blast could be heard 10 miles away and local houses within a mile's radius of the explosion had their windows shattered. Valiant rescue efforts were made by the boom defence vessel *Barfield* but a second explosion proved fatal and the best the rescuers could do was to ground the French ship on a nearby sandbank where she proved to be a local landmark for the next 20 years before being raised and removed. She carried a crew of 230 of whom 27 were killed.

Warrior (249NT). Tug.
Lost on 15th March 1941 when she hit a mine, in all probability this would have been a parachute mine laid under cover of the air raids of 13th & 14th March on Clydebank. Due to wartime security her sinking position is unknown.

Topaze (608NT). Trawler.
Built by Smiths Dockyard Co and hired by the Admiralty for wartime anti-submarine duties. She was lost in a collision with HMS *Rodney* (33,900 tons), a Nelson Class battleship on 20th April 1941. Sinking position unknown.

HMS *Vandal* (540DT). V Class coastal submarine.
Built by Vickers Armstrong in Barrow and launched November 1942. While undergoing sea trials with a crew from her makers on board she was mysteriously lost. It is only recently that a possible position for the stricken vessel has been found. 55°43.781' N, 005° 22.425' W, lying in approx. 69 metres of water within sight of Lochranza on the Isle of Arran. There is a memorial to HMS *Vandal* at Lochranza.

HMS *Dasher* (8,200NT) Archer Class escort aircraft carrier. Built originally as the American merchant ship *Rio*

Opposite. 30th April 1940: French destroyer *Maillé Brézé* is badly damaged and sinking after an accidental explosion during torpedo maintenance. Twenty-seven men were killed, many of whom were trapped below. (Copyright James Hall Collection @ Norman Burniston)

de Janeiro by the Sun Shipbuilding and Drydock Co., in Chester, Pennsylvania and launched on April 12th 1941. She was chosen as one of six merchant ships to be urgently converted for the Royal Navy to use as one of the escort carriers which were vitally needed in the Battle of the Atlantic. Tietjens and Lang Dry Dock Co., of Brooklyn carried out the conversion in three months. The RN estimate was six months. She served in 3 campaigns in the Atlantic, North Africa and the Arctic.

On 27th March 1943, while involved in aircraft landing exercises in the Clyde, she was engulfed in an enormous explosion which had a catastrophic result. Within eight minutes HMS *Dasher* sank stern first into 170 metres of water; 379 men lost their lives, while 149 survivors were rescued and taken to Ardrossan and Greenock. Due to strict wartime security and the Official Secrets Act, reports of the disaster were not released officially until 1973, and it was not until the 1990s that further details of her sinking were issued.

HMS *Untamed* (540DT) U Class submarine

Built by Vickers Armstrong, Newcastle upon Tyne and launched 8th December 1942. While exercising with ships of the 8th Escort Group off Campbeltown on 30th May 1943, after two successful dives, she failed to surface. A faulty sluice valve was the cause of the loss of the boat and her entire crew of 34, who were later buried at Dunoon Cemetery, South 3 Coll, Graves 26-50.

The *Untamed* was salvaged on 5th July 1943, refitted and renamed HMS *Vitality* returning to service in July 1944. She came off the active list in February 1946 and was later scrapped.

Left. HMS *Dasher* (Archer-Class Escort Carrier) sunk in the Clyde on the 27th March 1943 following a catastrophic explosion while on exercise. 379 men lost their lives. (Copyright *Daily Record*).

Far left. A view of the death throes of HMS *Dasher* as rescuers saved 149 survivors from the cold waters of the Clyde. (Copyright *Daily Record*).

APPENDICES

HMS *GLEANER*

Built by William Gray & Co on Tyneside, she was a Halcyon Class minesweeper. Her keel was laid on 17th June 1936, and she was launched on 10th June 1937, completing these nine months later on 30th March 1938. Originally designed as a survey ship, at the outbreak of war she was converted to a minesweeper in Plymouth. On completion she joined the 1st Anti-submarine Striking Force based at Belfast and patrolled the Irish Sea area.

By the end of the year she was operating with the 2nd Anti-submarine Striking Force, between the Clyde and Loch Ewe as the Home Fleet had been dispersed to these areas of safety after the sinking of the *Royal Oak* in Scapa Flow. In January 1940 she transferred to the 3rd Anti-submarine Striking Force based in the Clyde, where on 12th February 1940 she achieved her greatest triumph, the sinking of U-33.

In August 1940 she was detached from her minesweeping duties in the Clyde to become a member of the Northern Escort Force. In 1942 she was converted in Leith to a Fleet Minesweeper and fitted out for Arctic conditions. On completion she joined the 1st Minesweeping Flotilla, Home Fleet and escorted convoys

The White Ensign flies proudly and defiantly. (Copyright *Daily Record*).

between Scapa Flow and Ireland as well as the Kola Inlet.

On 25th August 1944 HMS *Gleaner* suffered extensive damage from a near miss with a mine whilst sweeping the area of Cap d'Antifer north of Le Havre. Repaired and put back into service in the Channel area, she was badly damaged in a collision with a pilot ship in March 1945. Again patched up she returned to 1st Minesweeping Flotilla until September 1946 when she was paid off into the naval reserve at Falmouth. On 12th May 1950 she was transferred to the ship breakers to end her career. A small ship, but she played a vital part in the winning of the war.

Prior to service on HMS *Gleaner*, Hugh Percival Price served on HMS *Herald* from 28th March 1935 as a Lieutenant Commander serving as second in command under Captain EFB Law. The *Herald's* home port was Devonport and is described in the 1935 Navy list as a surveying vessel of 1,650 tons. HMS *Gleaner* was also a Devonport ship and Price was appointed on 7th May 1937 as Lieutenant Commander in Command. His First Lieutenant was Sub. Lt EP Reade. Following the successful action against U-33 on 12th February 1940, the *London Gazette* announced on 24th April 1940 the award of the Distinguished Service Order (DSO) to Lt Cdr Hugh Percival Price, Sub. Lt Edward Perry Reade received the Distinguished Service Cross (DSC) and Mentioned in Despatches were Able Seaman Harold Thomas Rhodes SSS23375, Able Seaman William John Trevethan Mellor SSX23375 and Able Seaman Bernard Duncan Winstanley J115205.[12] In each case the citation read,

> For outstanding, readiness, proficiency and skill in destroying an enemy submarine.

Lt Commander HP Price had a distinguished war career and by October 1945 he was serving as a surveyor on the staff of the Hydrographer of the Navy and was employed at HMS President. This was the name for the Admiralty and all those serving in London were borne on the books of President. In January 1946, he was awarded the Order of the British Empire (OBE) in the New Year's Honours List. This award does not have an accompanying citation, the honour being presented for 'Good and Loyal and Faithful Service to the King.'

Hugh P Price retired from the Royal Navy in January 1947 and died in 1983. Sub. Lt Edward Perry Reade died 15th November 1966.

12 In terms of Military Awards, the Victoria Cross is the highest award with the DSO, DSM and CGM on the 2nd highest award band. The DSC, MC, DFC, DSM, MM, DFM are all on level three.

Above. RMS *Aquitania* (45,600t), a Cunard liner, in her wartime grey she appears like a grey ghost while anchored in the Clyde. She was built by John Brown and Co Ltd of Clydebank and launched on 21st April 1913. Her sister ships were the RMS *Mauritania* and RMS *Lusitania*. (Copyright Scottish Maritime Museum)

Opposite. Prime Minister Winston Churchill on board HMS *Prince of Wales* in August 1941 en route to Atlantic Charter Meeting in USA with President Roosevelt. Four months later the *Prince of Wales* was sunk by Japanese Dive Bombers in the South China Sea. (Copyright *Daily Record*)

The largest convoy to reach the Clyde safely sailed from Fremantle, Australia on the 4th May 1940 with 14,000 Australian and New Zealand troops. Convoy US 3 travelled via Capetown, South Africa and Freetown, Sierra Leone before reaching home waters. The convoy was escorted on the final leg by HMS *Hood* and a strong RN contingent. As well as the *Queen Mary* (81,000 tons), the convoy included the liners *Empress of Canada* (45,600 tons), *Aquitania* (45,600 tons), *Empress of Brotain* (42,300 tons), *Empress of Japan* (26,000 tons) later renamed *Empress of Scotland.* All these ships were Clyde-built. Accompanying them were the *Mauretania* (35,700 tons) built at Cammell Laird, Birkenhead in 1939 and the Andes (27,000 tons) built by Harland & Wolff in Belfast. The convoy arrived safely on the Clyde on the 16th June 1940 carrying the first contingent of Australian and New Zealand troops to arrive in Britain.

At the end of the war the following message was sent from 10 Downing Street, to the officers and men of the minesweeping flotillas.[13]

> Now that Nazi Germany has been defeated I wish to send to you all on behalf of His Majesty's Government a message of thanks and gratitude.
>
> The work you do is hard and dangerous. You rarely get and never seek publicity: your only concern is to do your job, and you have done it nobly. You have sailed in many seas and all weathers, with superior science and ingenuity you have rendered harmless ever kind of mine the enemy could devise, and you have swept the seas free of over 16,000 mines since the war began. This work could not be done without loss, and we mourn all who have died and over 250 gallant ships sunk on duty. No work has been more vital than yours: no work has been better done. The ports were kept open and Britain breathed. The Nation once again is proud of you.
>
> *Winston S. Churchill*

13 Source: National Archives PREM3/314/5

HMS *GLEANER*

HMS *Gleaner*, Halcyon Class Minesweeper
Built by W. Gray, West Hartlepool
Keel laid 17th June 1936. Launched 10th June 1937
Commissioned: 30th March 1938
Standard Displacement: 875 tons
Full Displacement: 1350 tons
Length: 245ft 9in
Beam: 33ft 6in
Draught: 9in
Endurance: 6,000nm at 10 knots; 4,800nm at 15 knots
Speed: 17 knots
Propulsion: Two Admiralty 3-drum boilers, two geared turbines driving two shafts at 2,000 hp
Complement: 80 (peacetime)
Armament: 2 x 4in AA, 4 x 0.5in, MG AA 4 x 0.303in MG, Anti Submarine 4 x Depth Charge Throwers, 2 x Depth Charge Rails
Pennant No: J 83
Number of Halcyon Class built: 2

DISTINGUISHED SERVICE ORDER (DSO)

Instituted in 1886, for officers, 'Who had rendered meritorious or distinguished service in War' this honour is awarded only to officers who have been mentioned in dispatches for their conduct in active operations. It is the reward for a unit commander who shows especially skilled and courageous leadership qualities in action. The blue-edged red ribbon of the enamelled cross recalls the ribbons of the army gold cross and other medals of the Napoleonic Wars.

DISTINGUISHED SERVICE CROSS (DSC)

This decoration was instituted in World War One for junior officers in the Royal Navy and awarded for 'gallant and distinguished services in action.' The typical award is to an officer who leads his men in battle with exceptional courage and resourcefulness. The ribbon on the DSC retains the Royal Navy's austere blue and white colours.

MENTIONED IN DISPATCHES

Servicemen of all ranks who distinguish themselves by some act of courage or skill which is not held to qualify them for the award of a higher honour, receive these commendations. They are awarded on the recommendation of the unit commander. The visible mark of this class of honour is an oak leaf insignia, which is worn sewn to the ribbon of the campaign medal relevant to the award.

ENIGMA CODING MACHINE

The German Armed Forces used a machine known as Enigma to encode all of their secret communications and they considered that it could not be deciphered. It was essentially a modified electric typewriter, initially using three rotors with 26 contacts each. Each rotor was wired to connect the 26 contacts in pairs in a different pattern. As the operator typed a letter on the keyboard, an electrical impulse was sent to the appropriate contact in the first rotor and output through the connected contact. This letter was then input to the second rotor and then to the third rotor. The final output showed as a light which appeared under one of the letters in a panel of letters in the pattern of a keyboard located above the input keys. As long as the receiver had the same rotors in reverse order, the message could then be decoded.

At the beginning of the Second World War, U-Boats had a coding machine which in addition to the sockets for three rotors, also had a sequence of ten jacks and plugs to give further variations to the circuitry. Each boat carried five extra rotors so that the various keys in which messages might be received could be handled. By varying the sequence of rotors and plugs, different keys could be read. The Polish Secret Service were aware of Enigma long before the war and their knowledge was passed on to the British in July 1939. British cryptographers, working at

The Enigma 3-rotor encoding machine similar to that provided to the Kreigsmarine in the early part of the Second World War. The design and capability was changed to a 4-rotor model in February 1942. (Copyright Nigel West)

Bletchley Park, reconstructed an Enigma machine and by mid-1941 were able to break the majority of the German codes. This breakthrough played a major part in the winning of the Battle of the Atlantic as well as other theatres of war. The first capture of parts of an Enigma machine in the Clyde in February 1940 led to the reconstruction of an Enigma machine at Bletchley Park and helped to break the Enigma code.

BLETCHLEY PARK

Located in the small English town of Bletchley, near Milton Keynes, the Government Code and Cipher School was established in 1939. The cryptographers working here during the war, penetrated and read vital amounts of Enigma- and Lorenz-enciphered German top-secret military and diplomatic traffic that was being transmitted by radio. It remained a closely guarded secret until well after the war. The work carried out at Bletchley, was vital in winning the war for Britain.

Right. Bletchley Park, headquarters of the Government Code and Cipher School. (Copyright www.frobenius.com)

KARL DÖNITZ

Gross Admiral: The Last Führer.

> I wanted to imbue my crews with enthusiasm and a complete faith in their arm and instill in them a spirit of selfless readiness to serve in it. Only those possessed of such a spirit could hope to succeed in

Far right. Karl Dönitz, leader of the U-boats and last Fuhrer of Germany.

Left. December 1945, 75 U-boats anchored in Loch Ryan prior to being sunk by the Royal Navy in the deep waters of the North Channel between Scotland and Northern Ireland. (Copyright James Hall Collection @ Norman Burniston)

> the grim realities of submarine warfare. Professional skill alone would not suffice. I believe in the fighting powers of the U-boat, I regarded it, as I have always regarded it, as a first-class weapon of offence in naval warfare.

Born in Berlin on 16th December 1891, Dönitz set out on his naval career in the Kaiserliche Marine in April 1910, graduating in Crew No 10 from naval college and joined his first ship, the cruiser SMS *Breslau* in 1913. For the early part of World War One she operated from Istanbul in Turkey, as the Turks were German allies in the eastern Mediterranean. In October 1916 Dönitz started his long U-Boat career, and in the final weeks of the war he received his first command, UC-25. After only six days in charge he was transferred to UB68 which he lost including six crew members, after some problems during a dive with an unstabilised boat. He then spent nine months in British captivity before returning to Germany and served the next 16 years in the Reichsmarine, mainly on torpedo boats before receiving command of the cruiser *Emden* in 1934. This ship was where future naval officers got their training in a year-long cruise round the world. When *Emden* returned to Wilhelmshaven, the Third Reich under Hitler was firmly established in power, and Grand Admiral Erich Raeder, Commander-in-Chief, gave Dönitz the order to immediately build up the German U-boat fleet. He started in September 1935 with three U-boats. On 1st January 1936 he was appointed Fuhrer der Unterseeboote (FdU) and on 19th September the title changed to BdU. Dönitz effectively became the 'Father of the U-boat', developing tactics, and was instrumental in setting up the 'Wolf Packs' to hunt down the Atlantic convoys.

The U-boats came close to winning the Battle of the Atlantic due to the skill and planning of Karl Dönitz. In 1943 he was made Commander-in-Chief of the

Opposite. 1939–45: Gourock and the Clyde with a convoy preparing for departure. (Copyright James Hall Collection @ Norman Burniston)

Overleaf. RMS *Queen Elizabeth* prepares to leave her birthplace at John Brown & Co Ltd yard at Clydebank to sail downriver to Greenock. On 2nd March 1940 she set off on her maiden voyage to New York unescorted. (Copyright James Hall Collection @ Norman Burniston)

Kreigsmarine but still retained his BdU title. A committed Nazi, he was named Fuhrer after Hitler's suicide until his capture by British Forces on 23rd May 1945. At the Nuremberg trials he was found guilty of war crimes and served 11 years in prison, the last 10 in Spandau Prison, Berlin. He lost two sons in the U-boat war and was released on 30th September 1956. He died on 24th December 1980.

RMS *QUEEN ELIZABETH*

On the 27th September 1938, HM Queen Elizabeth launched her namesake at John Brown & Co Ltd shipyard, Clydebank. Both the king and queen were due at the launch, but the king had to cancel due to the political situation in Europe.

At 83,673 tons *Queen Elizabeth* was the world's largest liner and was scheduled to maintain and enhance Cunard's transatlantic service along with RMS *Queen Mary*. Moved to the fitting-out basin, her interior was completed and the massive steam turbines that were capable of producing 32 knots, were installed. With the sinking of the U-33 in the early hours of 12th February 1940, five miles south-east of Arran, the authorities realised how vulnerable the *Queen Elizabeth* was, just 20 miles up the river from Greenock at Clydebank. Within two weeks, the giant liner slowly moved downstream to the crowded anchorage at Greenock. With a precedent-breaking lack of trial runs, she was handed over by the builders to Cunard, and on 2nd March 1940, with a skeleton crew of 398, she eased her way through the Cloch Boom and set off down the Firth of Clyde on what was to be a perilous maiden voyage. False rumours had been spread to confuse the enemy that she was making for Southampton but Captain John Townley, under sealed orders, proceeded at full speed for New York. After a five-day voyage, unescorted and steaming on a zig-zag course, the Clyde-built liner reached the safety of neutral America and New York where she received a partial fit-out throughout the summer of 1940 before leaving on 13th November and proceeding down the east coast of America via Trinidad to take on extra fuel and fresh water. As she was too big to go through the Panama Canal, she crossed the South Atlantic to Capetown, South Africa and across the vast expanse of the Indian Ocean to the key British base at Singapore before arriving at Sydney, Australia in February 1941, where she wasfinally converted fully into a troopship.

During the war, she sailed half a million miles, carrying over 750,000 troops and their supplies across the Atlantic contributing hugely to the war effort. *Queen Elizabeth* made 31 transatlantic round trips between Gourock and New York and three to Halifax, Nova Scotia.

At the end of hostilities, she was returned to passenger and mail service in the distinctive Cunard colours for the first time, after spending the war as a ghost-like grey ship. She made her maiden passenger voyage to New York on 16th October 1946. She was to remain the largest passenger ship in the world for the next 34 years before being withdrawn from service and sold. First she was moored as a floating hotel and museum in Port Everglades, Florida, but the new owners had financial difficulties and she was auctioned off to the highest bidder, a Taiwanese shipping

VS 3954

tycoon named CY Tung who wanted to turn her into a floating university. After many mechanical problems she finally arrived in Hong Kong, was then renamed *Seawise University*, and work started to bring her up to modern safety standards.

On 9th January 1972, five mysterious fires broke out through the ship. The fire protection system was incomplete and firefighting efforts were overwhelmed. She was now listing over on her starboard side and by the next morning had sunk and lay on her side at the bottom of Hong Kong harbour. There was no hope of salvage, and the once proud flagship of the Cunard Line was sold for scrap value. An ignominious end to a wonderful, graceful Clyde-built liner that had contributed immeasurably to the Allied war victory.

Left. A view from a wartime window in Gourock. Note the masking tape on the windows to prevent flying glass in the event of an air raid. (Copyright *Daily Record*).

Above. Off Arran RMS *Queen Elizabeth*, restored to her peacetime Cunard colours, after her wartime troopship duties, goes through her paces on the measured mile, with HM Queen Elizabeth and the two princesses on board, before entering transatlantic service on 16th October 1946. (Copyright Scottish Maritime Museum)

Right. HMS *Hood*, seen here undergoing full-power sea trials off Arran in 1920. She was Britain's largest warship at the outbreak of war in 1939. Twenty-two months later she was sunk in her first engagement with the Bismarck. (Copyright *Daily Record*)

Opposite left. A wounded survivor from the *Bismarck* is gently brought ashore at Gourock. (Copyright James Hall Collection @ Norman Burniston)

Opposite right. Argyll and Sutherland officers shepherd more *Bismarck* survivors on to the Glasgow-bound train at Gourock. (Copyright James Hall Collection @ Norman Burniston)

HMS *HOOD*

Designed in 1915, and built under the Emergency War Programme, her keel was laid down at John Brown & Co, Clydebank, on 1st September 1916 just four months after the Battle of Jutland and while heavy fighting continued on the Somme.

Originally four of these Admiral Class battlecruisers were planned, but after Jutland the threat from the German High Seas Fleet had evaporated and no more of the class were built. She was launched on 22nd August 1918 by Lady Hood, widow of Sir Horace Hood, who was lost at Jutland, and just three months before the Armistice and the end of World War One. It wasn't until 5th March 1920 that she was finally completed.

At 48,650 tons (full load) and carrying a complement of 1,400 men, she was the last of the British battlecruisers. She was the largest, fastest and most heavily armed capital ship in the world between 1920 and 1940. With eight 15-inch and eight four-inch guns plus anti-aircraft protection and capable of 30 knots, the *Hood* was a formidable ship, the true embodiment of British naval power. However the *Hood* had an Achilles heel, because of her design, in effect that of a World War One battlecruiser, deck armour had been sacrificed for speed and so her horizontal plating was inadequate to stop plunging enemy shell fire at long range.

As she neared completion at Clydebank in December 1919 she was visited by HRH Prince Albert (later HM King George VI) who had been a midshipman at Jutland. Commissioned at Rosyth after trials in the Clyde, on 15th

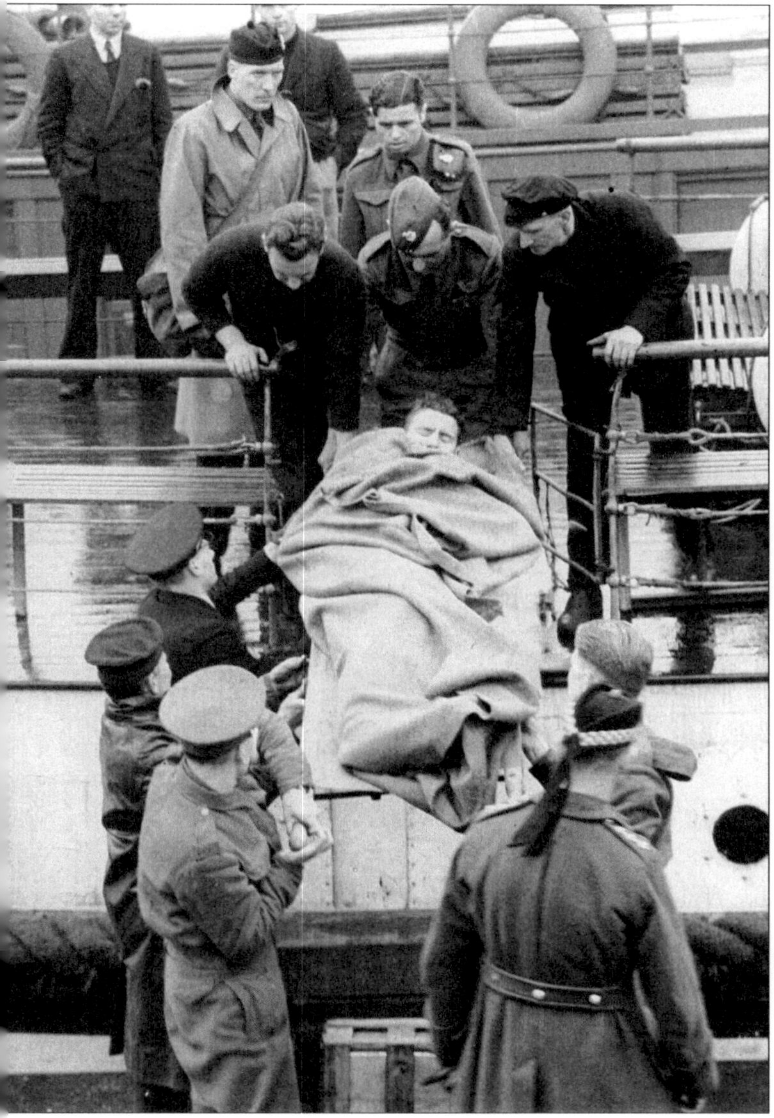

At Gourock Pier a wounded survivor from *Bismarck* comes up the gangway. (Copyright James Hall Collection @ Norman Burniston)

May 1920 HMS *Hood* was accepted by the Royal Navy as the flagship. Cruises to Scandinavia, the Mediterranean and the West Indies were regular features for a peacetime navy, but her greatest success was her world, or empire cruise from November 1923 to September 1924.

In 10 months, accompanied by HMS *Repulse* and five Light Cruisers she covered 38,000 miles and welcomed 750,000 visitors. Leaving Devonport the first stop was in Sierra Leone, then on to South Africa, next to Zanzibar before crossing the Indian Ocean to Ceylon (now Sri Lanka). Kuala Lumpur and Singapore were next on the itinerary before reaching Perth in Western Australia, Adelaide, Melbourne and Sydney completed a very successful Australian visit. A brief call at Hobart, Tasmania before New Zealand's Wellington and Auckland had their chance to view this unparalleled symbol of British sea power.

Fiji and Hawaii were brief stops on the way to Vancouver on Canada's West Coast before a courtesy call to San Francisco and then after a tight squeeze through the Panama Canal. Jamaica and the West Indies in the Caribbean provided a sunshine break, before turning northwards and the East Coast of Canada. Nova Scotia and Quebec were the last two ports of call before heading across the Atlantic to Devonport and home, the *Hood* and her squadron did a superb job for Britain. Her loss was felt throughout the empire.

After her world cruise, the next 10 years or so saw *Hood* having regular spring cruises in Spanish and Mediterranean waters, resulting in her being transferred to the

At a press conference in Greenock on their return from the action that saw the Royal Navy sink the Bismarck and avenge the loss of the *Hood*. Left to right: Capt FHG Dalrymple-Hamilton of HMS *Rodney* (battleship), Capt HC Bovell of HMS *Victorious* (aircraft carrier), Rear Admiral W. Wake-Walker of HMS *Norfolk* (Cruiser). (Copyright James Hall Collection @ Norman Burniston)

Mediterranean Fleet in 1936 due to the worsening situation in Spain and the imminent civil war there. There was a minor confrontation with Franco's navy in April 1937 but it came to nothing.

As the war clouds were looming, *Hood* was refitted and recommissioned in the Home Fleet in June 1939. On 17th September 1939 while at Loch Ewe, Churchill, then First Lord of the Admiralty and accompanied by Admiral Sir Charles Forbes, made his first wartime visit to the ship. Over the next six months Churchill made a further two visits to *Hood*, the first at Greenock on 31st October 1939 and later at Scapa Flow on 8th March 1940. In June 1940 she was allocated to Force H, and its first task was to neutralise the Vichy French squadron at Oran in Algeria. At 17.55 on 3rd July 1940 the *Hood* opened fire in anger for the first time as the British Fleet carried out a determined attack. The battleship *Bretagne* was blown up and the *Provence* and *Dunkerque* were badly damaged in this distasteful but necessary action. *Hood* returned to the Home Fleet and on the 16th March 1941, an inspection by HM King George VI was carried out at Rosyth, just 21 years after his first visit to the ship at Clydebank.

Two months later Vice Admiral Lancelot E. Holland, the new commander of the battlecruiser squadron and second-in-command of the Home Fleet, set up his flag command in *Hood*. Twelve days later he perished along with 1,414 of his crew in a short, disastrous battle with *Bismarck*. The *Hood* and the newly completed *Prince of Wales* (still with shipyard technicians on board) were dispatched to intercept the German battleship (at 50,153 the most powerful ship in the world) and the heavy battle-cruiser *Prinz Eugen* (18,200 tons).

May 27th 1941 and desperate survivors of the *Bismarck* are picked up by the Royal Navy. (Copyright *Daily Record*)

They met at first light on the morning of 24th May 1941 in the Denmark Strait between Iceland and Greenland. The *Bismarck*'s fifth salvo of long-range plunging fire hit the *Hood* on the upper deck, started a fire, which shortly afterwards caused a catastrophic explosion that blew the ship apart. Her position was 63° 21' N 31° 47' W and she left only three survivors.

Although the *Bismarck* was down at the bow and losing oil, the *Prince of Wales* had to break off the action. The German battleship then separated from the *Prinz Eugen* and began to head for an occupied French port and safety.

Because the *Hood* was held in such high esteem by the British public her sudden loss had a major impact on British morale and worldwide opinion. This was only assuaged by the sinking of the *Bismarck* three days later at 10.40am on 27th May 1941, after a fortuitous strike by a Swordfish torpedo plane from *Ark Royal* disabled the enemy battleship's rudder and delivered her to the avenging guns and torpedoes of the Royal Navy after one of the most dramatic chases in naval history.

Bismarck's sinking position was 48°10' N, 16°12' W. HMS *Hood* received only one battle honour, it reads:

BISMARCK, 1941

GLOSSARY

AA	Anti-Aircraft
ASDIC	Allied Submarine Detector Investigation Committee. Called 'Sonar' in America. A device for detecting submerged submarines.
B-Dienst	German Intelligence listening Interception Service. (Beobachtungsdienst)
BdU	Initials of Befelshaber der Unterseeboote Commander in Chief for Submarines
DT	Displacement Tonnage
FdU	Initials of Fuhrer der Unterseeboote Chief/Leader/Head/Commander of Submarines
GT	Gross Tonnage
HF/DF	High Frequency Direction Finding.
HMS	His/Her Majesty's Ship
Kaiserliche Marine	German Navy 1871–1919 (Imperial Navy)
Kapitanleutnant zur See	Lieutenant Commander
Knot	The speed of ships is measured in knots. One knot is one sea mile per hour (a sea mile is a little longer than a land mile)
Kreigsmarine	German Navy 1935–1945
NT	Net Tonnage
MGAA	Machine Gun Anti-Aircraft
Oberleutnant zur See	Lieutenant
Obersteurmann	German rating of warrant rank who carried out the duties of a navigating officer in a U-boat
TMB	German Acoustic Mine: 580kg charge to be used in depths not exceeding 25m.
TMC	Improved Acoustic Mine: 1000kg charge.
TT	Turn Two flak gun
RMS	Royal Mail Ship
SS	Steamship

BIBLIOGRAPHY

Admiralty publication, *Fuehrer Conferences on Naval Affairs 1939–45*, 1947. Foreword by JP Mallmann Showell

Dönitz, Admiral Karl, *Ten Years and Twenty Days*, Cassell & Co, 2000

Drummond, John D, *A River Runs to War*, WH Allen & Co Ltd, 1960

Farago, Ladilas, *The Game of the Foxes*, Hodder and Stoughton, 1972

Harris, Paul, *Glasgow at War, A Pictorial Account 1939–45*, Archive Publications, 1986

His Majesty's Stationery Office, *British Vessels lost at Sea 1939–45*, HMSO, 1947, reprinted 1977

Jeffrey, Andrew, *This Time of Crisis.*, Mainstream Publishing Company (Edinburgh) Ltd,1993

Kemp, Paul, *U-Boats Destroyed. German Submarine losses in the World Wars,* Arms & Arms Press, 1997

Lenton, HT and Colledge JJ, *Warships of World War II,* Ian Allan Publishing Ltd, 1972

Lwein, Ronald, *Ultra goes to War The Secret Story*, Hutchinson, 1978

Mallmann Showell, JP, *Enigma U-Boats Breaking the Code*, Ian Allen Publishing Ltd, 2000

Mallmann Showell, JP, *The German Navy in World War Two*, Arms & Arms Press, 1979

Mallmann Showell, JP, *U-Boats under the Swastika*, Ian Allen Publishing Ltd, 1973

Miller, David, *U-Boats, History, Development and Equipment*, Pegasus Publishing Ltd, 2000

Miller, William H & Hutchings, David F, *Transatlantic Liners at War,* David & Charles, Newton Abbot 1985

Ministry of Defence (Navy), *The U-Boat War in the Atlantic 1939–45*, Her Majesty's Stationery Office, 1989

Ministry of Information, *His Majesty's Minesweepers*, His Majesty's Stationery Office, 1943

Moir, Peter & Crawford, Ian, *Clyde Shipwrecks*, place of publication, Wemyss Bay, 1997 (2nd Edition)

Osborne, Brian D and Armstrong, Ronald, *The Clyde at*

War, Birlinn Ltd, Edinburgh 2001
Sebag-Montefiore, Hugh, *Enigma: The Battle for the Code,* Weidenfeld and Nicolson, 2000
Smith, Michael, *Station X The Codebreakers of Bletchley Park,* Channel 4 Books, 1998
Steele, John & Noreen, *The Secrets of HMS Dasher,* Argyll Publishing, Glendarual 1995
Stern, Robert C, *Type VII U-Boats,* Brockhampton Press, 1998
Tarrant, VE, *The U-Boat Offensive 1914–1945,* Cassell & Co, 1989
Taylor, Bruce, *The Battlecruiser* HMS *Hood An Illustrated Biography 1916–1941,* Chatham Publishing 2004
Williams, Andrew, *The Battle of the Atlantic the Allies,* Basic Books, 2003
Williamson, Gordon, *U-Boat Bases and Bunkers 1941–45,* Osprey Publishing, 2003

INDEX

Page numbers in *italics* indicate a map or photographs.